Emma
the Brave

Written and Illustrated by
Emma Marques

Interior Design by R'tor John D. Maghuyop
Illustrated by Emma Marques

CHALFANT ECKERT
PUBLISHING

1028 S Bishop Avenue, Dept. 178
Rolla, MO 65401

Printed in United States of America

Emma the Brave

Written and Illustrated by

Emma Marques

Emma would like to thank…

Her doctors and teams at
Memorial Sloan Kettering Cancer Center,
Weill Cornell Hospital,
The Ronald McDonald House New York,
Chalfant Eckert Publishing,
Books That Heal and Michael Flatley, and
All of her family and friends for their
love and support!

Emma the Brave is as brave
as brave can be
She is the bravest little girl
in New York City.
Emma is tiny but her strength
is off the charts.
What makes her so brave is the
size of her heart.

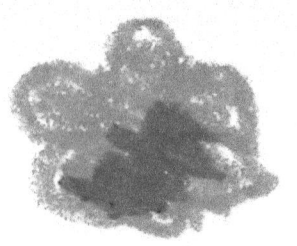
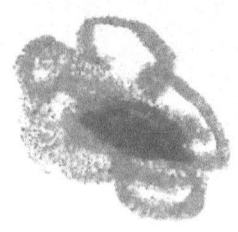

Emma flies to New York
to keep her strong.
This big city keeps her busy all day long.
She sees her doctors, but as soon as she's done
Emma is ready to explore the City
and have a lot of fun!

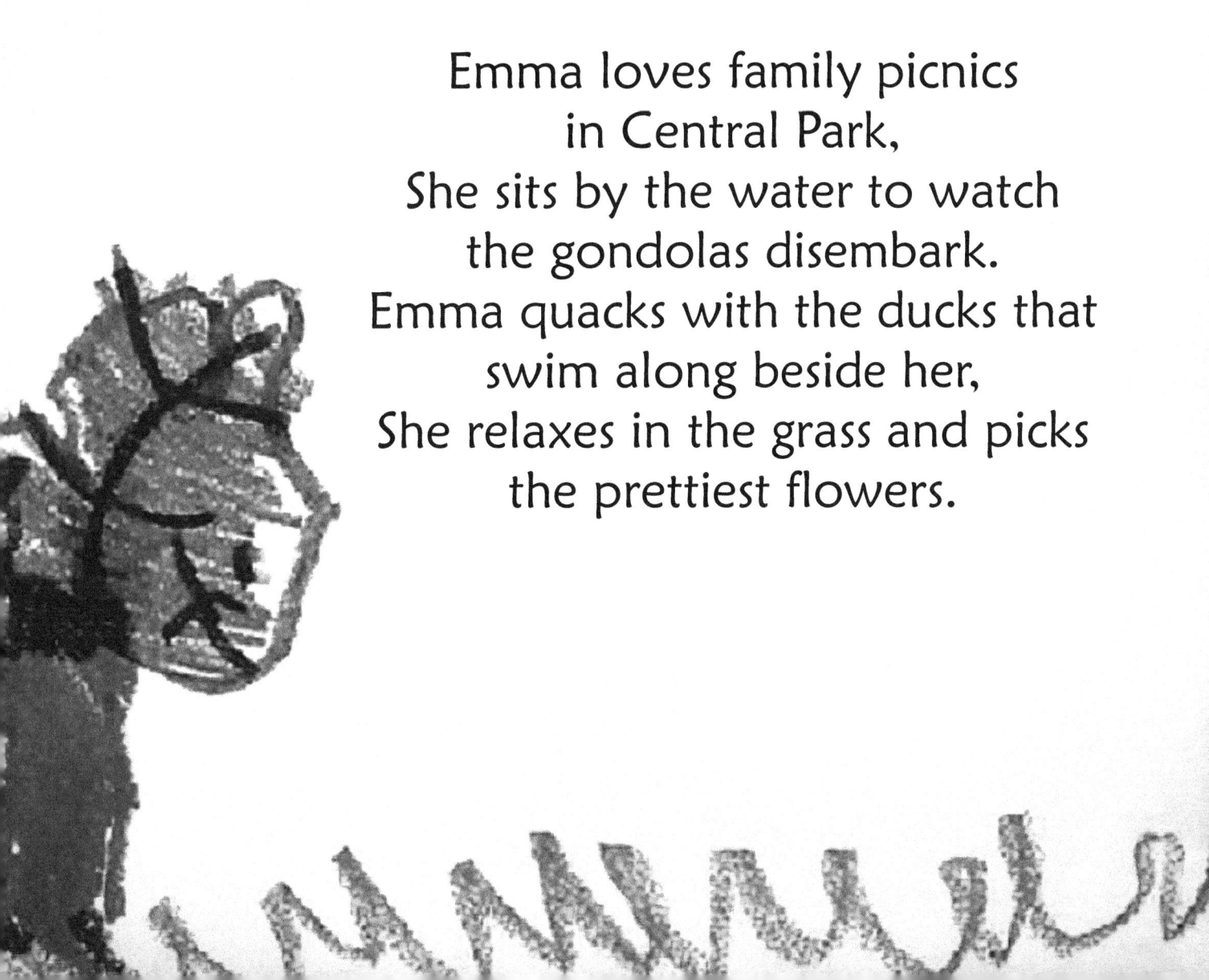

Emma loves family picnics
in Central Park,
She sits by the water to watch
the gondolas disembark.
Emma quacks with the ducks that
swim along beside her,
She relaxes in the grass and picks
the prettiest flowers.

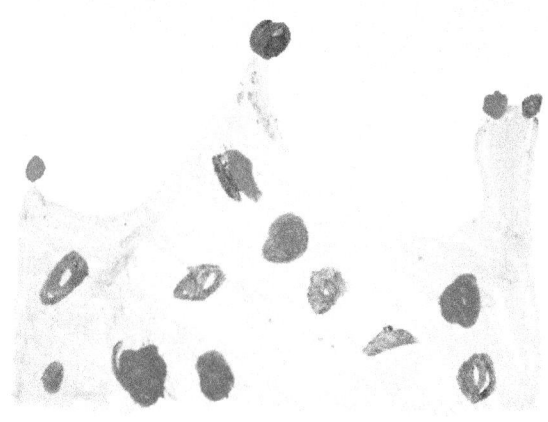

After relaxing in the Park,
Emma hails a taxi.
She's off to the Plaza Hotel
– it's time to be fancy!
Emma dresses up like a princess
and sips very elegant teas
With a pretty pink bow in her hair,
she looks just like Eloise.

Emma visits her doctors at least
five times a week,
She sits through her treatments
without even a peep.
Needles don't hurt Emma, not even a pinch,
Emma the Brave sits courageously
without even a flinch.

Emma loves to go to the Sweet Shop
that's across the street.
She opens the door and sees all
of her favorite treats.
The walls are filled with candies,
every color of the rainbow,
There is even a giant marshmallow!

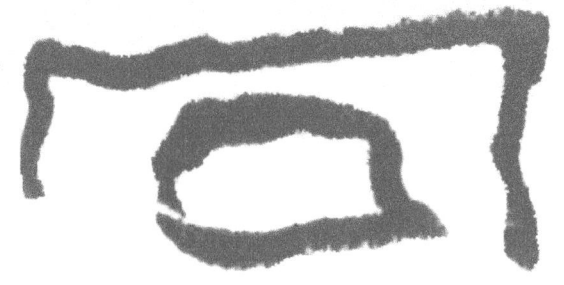

Back at the doctor's, Emma knows the deal:
The MRI machine takes pictures
of her to see how she feels.
The MRI's laser is very bright and red,
But **Emma the Brave** lays perfectly still and
does not even wobble her head.

American Girl Place

Emma finds time for a Rockefeller Center trip.
At the American Girl Store she can get her fix.
She can dress her American Girl
however she may please
And then have a tasty lunch,
filled with grilled cheese.

No trip to New York is complete until
Emma sees a Broadway play.
She's off to Times Square, not a second to delay!
The Rockettes, Matilda, and Cinderella
are all on scene.
What an amazing trip to New York it has been!

Emma is brave and you are brave, too.
You have your family's and friends'
love to help you through.
Whenever you are hurting and feel
like you're falling apart
Think of **Emma the Brave** – She's there
in your heart!

cure DIPG

100% of the proceeds raised from this book will go to the following organizations:

**Weill Cornell Brain and Spine Center
Children's Brain Tumor Project**
http://weillcornellbrainandspine.org/childrens-brain-tumor-project

Lily LaRue Foundation
www.Lilylaruefoundation.org

The Cure Starts Now Foundation
https://thecurestartsnow.org/heroes/view-heroes/200

Books That Heal
www.booksthathealcommunity.com

CPSIA information can be obtained
at www.ICGtesting.com
Printed in the USA
LVHW072143011019
632915LV00023B/177/P